GRANDPA'S HAMMER

GRANDPA'S HAMMER

Written by
RONALD KIDD

Illustrated by
BILL FARNSWORTH

A Habitat for Humanity Book

HABITAT FOR HUMANITY INTERNATIONAL
Americus, Georgia

To Paul Kidd and Lilli Loscutoff
—R.K.

To Allison, Maurice, Marie, Flora, and Dave,
who gave their time modeling for the characters in this book
—B.F.

Published by Habitat for Humanity International
121 Habitat Street
Americus, Georgia 31709-3498
1-800-422-4828

Millard Fuller • *President and Founder*
Joy Highnote • *Director, Product Development*
Joseph Matthews • *Director, Communication Services*

Edited, designed, and manufactured by
The Children's Marketplace
A division of Southwestern/Great American, Inc.
2451 Atrium Way, Nashville, Tennessee 37214
1-800-358-0560

Dave Kempf • *Vice President, Executive Editor*
Mary Cummings • *Managing Editor*
Ronald Kidd • *Project Editor*
Bruce Gore • *Book Design*

ISBN 1-887921-01-X
Library of Congress Catalog Number 95-61543

Manufactured in the United States of America
First printing: 1995

But someone will say, "You have faith and I have works."
Show me your faith without your works,
and I will show you my faith by my works.

James 2:18

This is Grandpa's hammer.

It has a round, flat head for hitting nails. It has two prongs on the back for taking them out. It has a smooth wooden handle.

When Grandpa holds the hammer, it is like part of his hand.

Grandpa uses his hammer to make things.
The things start out as dreams.
Grandma's kitchen table was a dream. So
was her rocking chair. So was my dollhouse.
Grandpa's hammer made them real.

I asked Grandpa how he knew what the
things would look like. He said it took faith.
Faith is believing in something you can't see.

Grandpa said it takes two things to make
dreams come true: faith and a hammer.

Then one day, Grandpa stopped
making things. It was the day Grandma died.
I missed my Grandma. I still do. But
Grandpa missed her even more.

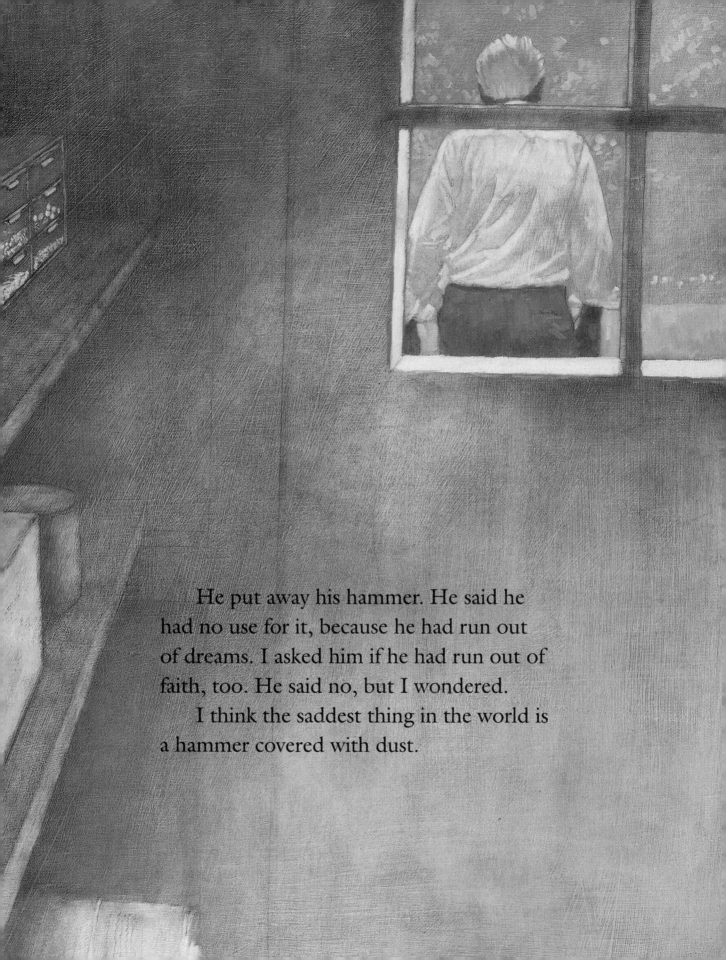

He put away his hammer. He said he
had no use for it, because he had run out
of dreams. I asked him if he had run out of
faith, too. He said no, but I wondered.
     I think the saddest thing in the world is
a hammer covered with dust.

I knew Grandpa was lonely, so I tried to make him feel better.

I made cookies for him. I took him on a walk. I gave him a hug. Nothing seemed to help.

I read him a story. It was called "Noah's Ark." I thought he might like the part where Noah builds a boat.

Grandpa never even looked up.

When I finished reading, there was a
knock at the door.

It was Mrs. Clark, a woman from down
the street. She asked Grandpa if she could
borrow his hammer for the day. He just
nodded.

I took her to the workshop and gave her the hammer. That afternoon, she brought it back. I was happy to see someone using it.

Grandpa didn't seem to care.

The next week she borrowed the hammer again. When she returned it, Grandpa looked at her but didn't say anything.

Each week, Mrs. Clark came back.
And each week Grandpa grew a little more
curious. Finally he asked, "What are you
doing with that hammer?"

"If you'll come along, I'll show you,"
she said.

At first he wasn't sure he wanted to go.
Then I took his hand, and we got into the
car with Mrs. Clark.

She drove us across town. There, in a field, people were working.

They had poured a concrete base. On top of it they were putting boards for the walls, doors, and windows. It wasn't finished yet, but I could see what it was going to be.

They were building a house.

"Who are these people?" asked Grandpa.

"They're from my church," said Mrs. Clark. "This is our work project."

She pointed to a man and woman sawing boards. "Those are the people who will live in the house when it's finished. Their names are Mr. and Mrs. Lewis."

Mrs. Clark said the project was started by Habitat for Humanity, a group that works in countries all around the world.

Habitat looks for families who don't have a decent place to live, then helps them build a new house for themselves. When the house is finished, the family often helps other families build Habitat houses.

Each family works side by side with Habitat helpers, such as Mrs. Clark and her church group. The helpers are called *volunteers*. They don't get paid. They work on the houses because they want to help people.

We stood there for a long time, watching the people work. Finally Grandpa said, "Do you think you could use some help?"

"We sure could," said Mrs. Clark. She gave his hammer back and said, "You may be needing this. I'll find another one."

It's been a year now since Grandma died. I know Grandpa misses her, but he's not lonely anymore. He's too busy.

Every Saturday, he works with other volunteers on Habitat houses. He's already helped to build ten of them.

Grandpa tells me he's doing a lot more than building houses. He's making dreams come true.

Anybody can do it, he says. It takes just two things: faith and a hammer.

RONALD KIDD is the author of thirty books for young readers and five plays. He received the Children's Choice Award and was nominated for the Edgar Allan Poe Award. Two of his plays were selected for development at the Eugene O'Neill Theater Center's National Playwrights Conference. He lives with his wife in Nashville, Tennessee.

BILL FARNSWORTH is a graduate of the Ringling School of Art and a member of the Society of Illustrators. His work has appeared in such publications as *Reader's Digest, Tennis Magazine, Golf Digest,* and *Field & Stream.* Recent books include *The Illustrated Children's Bible, Grandpa Is a Flyer,* and the forthcoming *Christmas Menorahs.* He lives in New Milford, Connecticut, with his wife Deborah and their two daughters, Allison and Caitlin.

Habitat for Humanity International
121 Habitat Street
Americus, Georgia 31709-3498

For more information, please call
1-800-HABITAT